BACKYARD BIRDS!

A MY INCREDIBLE WORLD PICTURE BOOK

MY INCREDIBLE WORLD

There are many different species
of birds that can be found
right in your own backyard!

MOURNING DOVE

Mourning Doves are often seen scavenging for seeds below bird feeders and plants.

DOWNY WOODPECKER

The smallest of all woodpeckers, the Downy pecks wood to make nests, find food and communicate!

AMERICAN ROBIN

American Robins are **omnivorous**, eating everything from worms and insects to nuts, berries and fruit!

AMERICAN CROW

American Crows are incredibly intelligent, and are able to solve problems and even use tools!

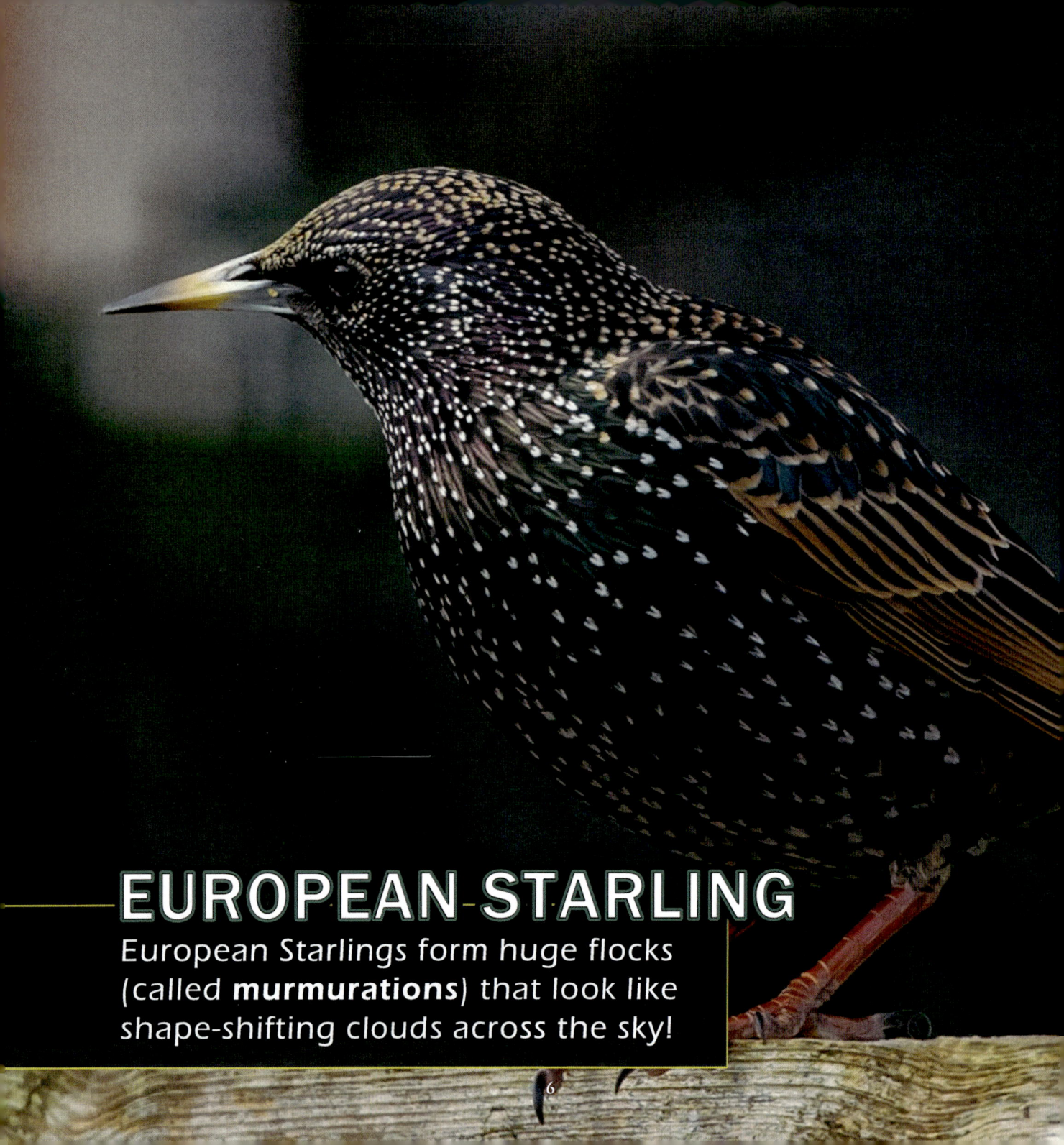

EUROPEAN STARLING

European Starlings form huge flocks (called **murmurations**) that look like shape-shifting clouds across the sky!

HOUSE SPARROW

House Sparrows live in organized groups, where the male with the biggest black patch is the leader!

HOUSE FINCH

House Finches feed their new babies plants almost exclusively, a rarity in the bird world!

AMERICAN-GOLDFINCH

Only the male American Goldfinch (a subspecies of House Finch) becomes bright yellow during breeding times.

BLUE JAY

Blue Jay feathers aren't actually blue; they just look it due to a cool light-scattering phenomenon!

NORTHERN CARDINAL

The Northern Cardinal is the most common official state bird, with 7 states naming it their own!

MOCKINGBIRD

Mockingbirds are great at **mimicry**, imitating the sounds of other birds, machines, objects and even humans!

CEDAR WAXWING

A group of Cedar Waxwings is called an **ear-full** or a **museum**!

BLACK-CAPPED CHICKADEE

Black-capped Chickadees are famous for hiding and storing food for later!

KILLDEER

Killdeer are known to pretend to have a broken wing in order to lure predators away from their nests.

HUMMINGBIRD

Hummingbirds can flap their wings more than 50 times per second!

BLUEBIRD

Bluebirds have amazing eyesight and can see insects from 60 feet away!

RED-WINGED BLACKBIRD

Red-winged Blackbirds puff up their feathers and sing to defend their home or attract a mate!

NUTHATCH

Nuthatches climb and cling onto tree trunks and branches upside down!

ORIOLE

Orioles have a sweet tooth and are easy to attract to your yard with oranges and grape jelly!

HOUSE WREN

House Wren males start building several nests to attract a mate, and females choose which one to finish!

Backyard birds are incredible!

Made in the USA
Las Vegas, NV
11 February 2025

18001416R00017